All rights reserved. This book or any portion thereof may not be reproduced or used in any manner whatsoever without the express written permission of the author except for the use of brief quotations in a book review.

Unless otherwise noted, all Scripture quotations are taken from the NEW KING JAMES VERSION ®. Copyright © 1982 by Thomas Nelson, Inc.
Used by permission. All rights reserved.

Emboldening, underlining, and italics within Scripture quotations are the author's emphasis.

Good News!

INTRODUCTION:
When was the last time you heard some really "GOOD NEWS"?

With the growth of the internet, and with the emergence of the 24/7 news cycle, we all receive a constant barrage of **"Bad News!"** Sure, occasionally there is the hint of some good news, but then that is quickly overshadowed by the next bad thing that happens.

We all could use some "GOOD NEWS!"

However, have you ever noticed that most good news is only temporary and that it really doesn't have the power to change our lives? What if there was some **"Good News"** that could not only brighten your day, *but it could also change the way you live and view your entire life!*

Wouldn't you want to hear this? "GOOD NEWS"

If you answered **YES!** - then you are just the person I want to talk to. The **"Good News"** that I want to share with you is **the oldest story ever told**, and yet, it is **the newest story you could ever hear.** It has been dismissed, misunderstood, and vehemently rejected by many.

Good News!

Yet, for countless individuals, this "Good News" has forever changed their lives!

*And here is a promise
that you can take to the bank!*

*This "GOOD NEWS"
could change your life too!*

The **"Good News"** I am referring to is found in the **Bible.** It is not found simply in a single verse of the Bible. Rather, it is found in *the complete story of the Bible -* from the opening book of **Genesis** to the closing book of **Revelation**. Therefore, the title of this book is,

*"GOOD NEWS
The Gospel of Jesus Christ,
from Genesis to Revelation!"*

I first shared this **"Good News"** while I did pre-marital counseling with couples. Later, I shared it as a message with our church family on a Sunday morning that we recorded and distributed on CDs.

Now, I am excited to be sharing this message with it you in this new format.

Good News!

The style of this book is "**conversational.**" I want you to imagine that we are having a personal conversation over a cup of coffee.

So, wherever you are, grab a cup of coffee, or your favorite beverage, and let's take some time together to explore **the great message of the Bible**, the...

"GOOD NEWS!"

Pastor Kirk

Good News!

TABLE of CONTENTS

- **INTRODUCTION:**
- **CHAPTER 1: Have you heard the Good News?**
- **CHAPTER 2: It All Started in A Garden.**
- **CHAPTER 3: The World's Most Misunderstood Tree.**
- **CHAPTER 4: Choices… Choices… Choices!**
- **CHAPTER 5: When Innocence Is Lost.**
- **CHAPTER 6: Is This Precious Baby A Sinner?**
- **CHAPTER 7: What Happens When We Sin?**
- **CHAPTER 8: What Is Death?**
- **CHAPTER 9: Where Is the Good News?**
- **CHAPTER 10: Who Can Conquer Death?**
- **CHAPTER 11: A New Baby Is Born!**
- **CHAPTER 12: We All Need A Blood Transfusion!**
- **CHAPTER 13: A Parking Meter…Or A Lifetime Pass?**
- **CHAPTER 14: PAID IN FULL!**

Good News!

- **CHAPTER 15: How Can We Overcome Sin and Death?**
- **CHAPTER 16: Why Do So Many People Miss the Free Gift?**
- **CHAPTER 17: Believing and Receiving Are More Than Just Saying A Prayer!**
- **CHAPTER 18: The "Doorknob" Is Repentance!**
- **CHAPTER 19: Repentance Must Be Followed with Surrender!**
- **CHAPTER 20: Surrender Is Lived Out Through Confession!**
- **CHAPTER 21: Jesus Is Knocking! Can You Hear It?**
- **EPILOGUE: Your Blessed Assurance of Salvation!**
- **ABOUT THE AUTHOR: Kirk L. Zehnder**
- **ACKNOWLEDGMENTS:**

Good News!

CHAPTER 1

"But as it is written: "Eye has not seen, nor ear heard, Nor have entered into the heart of man The things which God has prepared for those who love Him." I Corinthians 2:9

Have You Heard the "Good News?"

I would like to share with you what the Bible refers to as - the **"Gospel."** The Bible was originally written in the Greek language. The word "Gospel" in the Greek language literally means **"Good News."** As we study the Bible, we will discover that the Gospel is the **"Good News"** of God's plan of salvation for mankind through Jesus Christ. This **"Good News"** is the main theme of the entire Bible and can be found throughout every book of the Bible, from Genesis to Revelation.

Would you like to hear this "GOOD NEWS?"

When I first entered the ministry, I was the pastor of a small church in Mt. Baldy, California. As the new pastor, I inherited seventeen weddings that were scheduled on

Good News!

the church calendar. I felt that I had to do more than just perform wedding services, so I met with each couple for three or four, one-hour sessions. The first thing I did when I met with them was simply to share the **"Gospel" (Good News)** with them.

What I discovered is that most people had never really heard the **"Gospel."** I learned that many people, even though they grew up in church, didn't really understand the "**Gospel**" - *The Good News of Salvation in Jesus Christ.*

Many had heard preachers talk about Jesus. They were told that they needed to accept Jesus into their heart. Many were familiar with the story about how Jesus had died on the cross. And many had heard that if they did not believe in Jesus Christ, they could not have a relationship with God, and would not go to Heaven. However, they didn't understand what all of this really meant. They really did not understand why a relationship

Good News!

with Jesus Christ was so important. They were left with more questions than answers.

Why did Jesus have to die? Why did Jesus have to shed His blood? What does it mean to believe in Jesus? Can this **"Good News"** really change my life? These are the questions we want to answer as we look at the -

"**GOOD NEWS** - *The Gospel of Jesus Christ from Genesis to Revelation!*"

Good News!

CHAPTER 1 REVIEW

ASK YOURSELF THESE QUESTIONS

1. What do you think of when you hear **the word Gospel?**
2. Has anyone ever **shared the Gospel** with you?
3. When you die do you believe that you will **go to heaven? Why?**
4. What do **Jesus' life, death, and resurrection** have to do with the Gospel message?
5. Is your understanding of the Gospel really making a **dynamic change in your daily life?**

Good News!

CHAPTER 2

"In the beginning God created the heavens and the earth." Genesis 1:1

It All Started in a Garden

Let's begin by looking at the first book of the Bible, Genesis. In Genesis, we learn that God created man without sin. This is where the Good News begins. In Genesis 1:27- 31 we read;

> *"...Then God saw everything that He had made,* (including man and woman) *and indeed, **it was very good**. So, the evening and the morning were the sixth day."*

In Genesis 2:9, and then also in 2:15-16 we read,

> *"...Then the Lord God took the man and put him in the **Garden of Eden** to tend it and keep it. And the Lord God commanded*

Good News!

the man saying, "Of every tree of the garden you may freely eat."

God created both man and woman and He said that they were very good. This new man and woman were placed by God into a perfect environment called the Garden of Eden.

How many times have you found yourself looking for your own Garden of Eden? We try to make our backyards into our own personal oasis. We look for vacation spots where we can forget everything, sit under the palm trees, and gaze upon the beautiful blue ocean. We are all looking for a place where we can find total peace and harmony.

Why do we do this? The Bible tells us that inside each one of our hearts God has placed **eternity** – a craving for the very thing that was lost when Adam and Eve sinned in the Garden of Eden.

Good News!

> *"I have seen the God-given task with which the sons of men are to be occupied. He has made everything beautiful in its time. **Also, He has put eternity in their hearts,** except that no one can find out the work that God does from beginning to end."* Ecclesiastes 3:10-11

We all want it. We want the "fountain of youth." We want eternity. We want our own personal Garden of Eden. This is true for both Christians and non-Christians alike.

Many today are trying to achieve a certain level of accomplishment and awareness so that they can experience a deeper sense of purpose and peace. This points back to man's original desire – to return to his life in the Garden of Eden.

God created man to live in the Garden of Eden eternally blessed. When the Lord placed Adam and Eve in the

Good News!

garden, He gave them a wide variety of foods, and He gave them complete freedom - except for one thing, He said;

> "Here's one tree - the Tree of the Knowledge of Good and Evil - you cannot eat of that tree." Genesis 2:17 (*my paraphrase*)

Good News!

CHAPTER 2 REVIEW

ASK YOURSELF THESE QUESTIONS

1. What stands out in your mind regarding **God's creation of man and woman?**
2. What does **free will** mean to you? What did it mean to Adam and Eve?
3. What is your idea of the perfect **Garden of Eden** for your life?
4. Is your pursuit of this idea producing **purpose and peace** in your life?
5. Can you sense a **longing for eternity** in your life?

Good News!

CHAPTER 3

"The LORD God planted a garden eastward in Eden, and there He put the man whom He had formed. And out of the ground the LORD God made every tree grow that is pleasant to the sight and good for food. The tree of life was also in the midst of the garden, and the tree of the knowledge of good and evil." Genesis 2:8-9

The World's Most Misunderstood Tree

We have all seen commercials where the Tree of the Knowledge of Good and Evil is portrayed as an apple tree. No one really knows what kind of fruit was on this tree. It will be very interesting when we get to Heaven to find out what it really was.

What is the significance of this tree and its fruit? I don't believe there was anything mystical or magical about this tree. I also don't believe there was anything radiating from the fruit. The fruit itself did not hold an innate source of power. When they ate this fruit, they did not -

Good News!

"BOOM" – find something magical happening to them. The significance of this tree was none of the above. Yet, it was profoundly much more than all of the above.

Adam and Eve had just been invited to live in sinless perfection and harmony with the Creator of the Universe. They had the opportunity to live in total bliss and fulfillment for all eternity - IF they would simply follow and obey Him. Genesis 2:17 says,

> "But of the tree of the knowledge of good and evil **you shall not eat**, for in the day that you eat of it you shall surely die."

This tree was a test of their obedience and willingness to live in submission under God's rule, His Lordship. Lordship simply defines His rule, His care, and His direction for His creation. It also was a symbol of the gift to mankind of free will and free choice. You see, God wants us (just like any parent wants his child), to come to

Good News!

Him and love Him freely. Love demands both the freedom of choice and freedom of will (action).

Recently, during one of our Sunday morning services, as we gathered together in individual prayer circles, my daughter came up to me and gave me a hug and a kiss. It truly blessed me. Now, I don't want her to give me a hug and a kiss because I have said, "Every Sunday morning you will give me a hug and a kiss!" What significance would that hold? Yet, what a blessing it is when actions like these flow from spontaneity and her own free will. This is when it truly means something.

God wanted man and woman to serve Him willingly, freely, joyfully - as <u>their choice</u>. So, the tree represents that gift of free will, that gift of free choice. We all know the rest of the story. Man did not choose wisely.

Good News!

CHAPTER 3 REVIEW

ASK YOURSELF THESE QUESTIONS

1. What was the significance of the **Tree of Knowledge of Good and Evil**?

2. What does the term **Lordship** mean to me?

3. What does **true love** demand?

4. How do you see God's gift of **free will** working in your life?

5. What **does God desire** from everyone?

Good News!

CHAPTER 4

"I call heaven and earth as witnesses today against you, that I have set before you life and death, blessing and cursing; therefore choose life, that both you and your descendants may live; that you may love the LORD your God, that you may obey His voice, and that you may cling to Him, for He is your life and the length of your days…". Deuteronomy 30:19-20a

Choices…Choices…Choices

And so, the Gospel continues. We now encounter mankind's fall into sin. In Genesis 3:1-7 we read about Adam and Eve's life-changing choice.

> *"Now the serpent was more cunning than any beast of the field which the LORD God had made. And he said to the woman, '**Has God indeed said**, "You shall not eat of every tree of the garden"?'*

Good News!

And the woman said to the serpent, 'We may eat the fruit of the trees of the garden; but of the fruit of the tree which is in the midst of the garden, God has said, "You shall not eat it, nor shall you touch it, lest you die."'

*Then the serpent said to the woman, 'You will not surely die. For God knows that in the day you eat of it your eyes will be opened, and **you will be like God**, knowing good and evil.'*

So, when the woman saw that the tree was good for food, that it was pleasant to the eyes, and a tree desirable to make one wise, she took of its fruit and ate. She also gave to her husband with her, and he ate. Then the eyes of both of them were opened, and they knew that they were

Good News!

> *naked; and they sewed fig leaves together and made themselves coverings."*

The bottom line of the account found in Genesis chapter 3 is this – Satan, in the form of a serpent, came and said to them…

> "I'll tell you what, God's just pulling your leg. He really just wants you to be His personal puppet. He doesn't want to share His wisdom and His knowledge with you. You can be your own boss, you can be your own lord, and you can run your own life. ***If you just eat of this fruit, you'll have it all.*** God doesn't want to share it with you. So, go ahead, be your own boss! Call your own shots! Get in the driver's seat! Don't let God drive (direct your life) anymore! Wouldn't it feel good to be your own boss?" *(Personal Dramatization)*

Good News!

And so, Eve and Adam both ate of the forbidden fruit. They made the <u>wrong choice</u>.

Good News!

CHAPTER 4 REVIEW

ASK YOURSELF THESE QUESTIONS

1. Do I believe that **Satan is real?** (Both in the present and in this account from Genesis.)
2. How did Satan **entice Adam and Eve to disobey** God and eat from the forbidden tree?
3. How does Satan **entice me to disobey** God?
4. Adam and Eve made the wrong choice. **What wrong choices** have I made in my life?
5. How have these wrong choices **impacted my life** and current situation?

Good News!

CHAPTER 5

"As it is written: "There is none righteous, no, not one; There is none who understands; There is none who seeks after God. They have all turned aside; They have together become unprofitable; There is none who does good, no, not one." Romans 3:10-12

When Innocence is Lost

The Bible says when Adam and Eve ate of the forbidden fruit - all of a sudden, their eyes were opened. They looked at each other and they realized that they were naked. Why is this significant?

Before Adam and Eve sinned, they were clothed in the glory of God. After they sinned, they forfeited God's glory, which was the manifestation of His goodness, presence, and His love and rule over their lives. They instantly became aware of evil and their own inadequacies, weaknesses, and failures. They became aware of their nakedness!

Good News!

Do you remember when you were a child and you were innocent? Let me illustrate this. I believe you will get the picture.

I remember one time when all my childhood friends were doing obscene gestures with their hands. It was a common obscene gesture, and everyone was learning how to do it. However, I didn't know how to do it. I was innocent. But, because all my friends were doing it, I wanted to do it too! So, they had me train my hand using a pencil to get my hand positioned properly for doing this obscene gesture.

I will never forget what happened next. After I had learned how to do this with my hand, my hand would automatically go into that obscene gesture whenever I wanted it to. Suddenly, there was a wave of guilt that came over me. I wished that I didn't know how to do it. I didn't want my hand to know how to do it. I wanted my hand to go back to the way it was when it was innocent

Good News!

before I knew how to make that gesture. I had lost my innocence, and all of a sudden, I realized – **"I was naked."** Do you understand what I'm saying?

Adam and Eve's nakedness was the symbol that they had lost their innocence and the blessedness of living eternally in a state of perfection with God, the Creator of the universe. They now had entered into sin. Since that fateful day, sin has passed on to all mankind, from generation to generation. We are now sinners by nature. And we prove this fact by our actions.

Good News!

CHAPTER 5 REVIEW

ASK YOURSELF THESE QUESTIONS

1. What were Adam and Eve **clothed in** before they made the wrong choice?
2. What was the significance of Adam and Eve's **realization that they were naked?**
3. Can you remember the moment in your life when **you lost your innocence?**
4. How did this **make you feel?**
5. What is the evidence that Adam and Eve's fateful choice **has affected you** (and everyone), from that day forward?

Good News!

CHAPTER 6

"Behold, I was brought forth in iniquity, and in sin my mother conceived me." Psalms 51:5

Is This Precious Baby a Sinner?

I will never forget the day my daughter was born, and I held her in my arms for the first time! I looked at this wonderful, beautiful little package, and I thought to myself, "Nothing bad can ever come out of this beautiful little life - she's perfection!"

When my beautiful little daughter was about two years old, she started to defy and test both her mother and me. When she started to defy us, her sin nature, the ability to do what's wrong, all of a sudden activated – automatically! Her mother and I looked at each other and said, "Where did this stuff come from?" We knew the answer. It came from her mom, and it came from me. We had passed down to our daughter the sin nature we were born with.

Good News!

So, Adam and Eve forfeited the blessing they had received in the garden. The significance of the tree was "free will." They both exercised their freewill incorrectly. They entered into sin, and that "sin nature" (the propensity to sin) now dwelt within them. This "sin nature" has been passed down to all of their offspring, including you and me.

Good News!

CHAPTER 6 REVIEW

ASK YOURSELF THESE QUESTIONS

1. Was I born **inherently good** *or* **inherently bad?**
2. Do I believe that every child is born with a **sinful nature?**
3. When did I first recognize **my propensity to sin**, and the propensity of **my children to sin?**
4. How has sin **impacted my life?**
5. How has sin impacted the **life of my children?**

Good News!

CHAPTER 7

"For the wages of sin is death, but the gift of God is eternal life in Christ Jesus our Lord." Romans 6:23

What Happens When We Sin?

God had told Adam and Eve that if they ate of the Tree of Knowledge of Good and Evil – *"…they would surely die…"* (Genesis 2:17). The penalty for Adam and Eve's sin (their willful disobedience) **was death**. The Bible tells us that **all** men will face death. Ecclesiastes 8:8 says,

> *"No one has power over the spirit to retain the spirit, **and no one has power in the day of death**. There is no release from that war, and wickedness will not deliver those who are given to it."*

Hebrews 9:27 says,

> *"And as it is **appointed for men to die once**, but after this the judgment."*

Good News!

(For those who believe in reincarnation, this is bad news, but it is the truth.)

You live once, you die once, and then you are judged. There is no reincarnation. All men die. You and I will die. We cannot escape it.

Good News!

CHAPTER 7 REVIEW

ASK YOURSELF THESE QUESTIONS

1. When did the **penalty of death** begin?
2. What do you think of when you read – **"…the wages of sin is death?"**
3. Does the Bible teach the **possibility of reincarnation?**
4. **Finish this sentence** – "We live once, we die once, and then we are _____."
5. Am I **prepared to die?**

Good News!

CHAPTER 8

"So it was that the beggar died and was carried by the angels to Abraham's bosom. The rich man also died and was buried. And being in torments in Hades, he lifted up his eyes and saw Abraham afar off, and Lazarus in his bosom." Luke 16:22-23

What is Death?

As we study the Bible, we learn that death is both physical and spiritual. When a person dies, they do not simply cease to exist, their life goes on.

Jesus often taught in parables (an earthly story conveying a spiritual or heavenly truth). When He taught in parables, He never gave personal names to individuals. In Luke 16:20-31 Jesus speaks about a rich man and a poor man named Lazarus. He spoke about this poor person **by name**. So, we can conclude that this was not a parable. This was a true story!

Good News!

Jesus speaks about how both men died and how they both went to Hades (the name that is used in the Old Testament for the abode of the dead). On one side of Hades, in torment, was the rich man, who had lived his life for himself, and did not serve the Lord or others. On the other side was "Abraham's bosom" (this was the abode of the faithful awaiting the coming of Messiah, before Christ's death and resurrection). Dwelling in peace in "Abraham's bosom" was Lazarus. Lazarus, although poor, had both faithfully honored and served the Lord and others. Both the rich man and Lazarus were alive in the spirit. One was alive in torment, the other was alive and being comforted.

So, from this "true life" account we discover the stark reality - when we die physically, we do not die spiritually. We do not cease to exist. We continue to live eternally in the presence of God, or eternally in torment.

Good News!

So, what is "death"? Death is the separation of the body from the spirit. When a person dies his spirit is either separated or united with God throughout all eternity. They continue to exist either in God's presence or excluded from His presence.

This is what death is.

Good News!

CHAPTER 8 REVIEW

ASK YOURSELF THESE QUESTIONS

1. What is my **concept of death?**
2. What does the **Bible teach about death?**
3. From the story of the rich man and Lazarus, **what were the two different experiences** that each one had?
4. What happens to **my spirit when I die?**
5. Is death the **cessation of existence** or the entrance into a **new eternal existence?**

Good News!

CHAPTER 9

"For I know the thoughts that I think toward you, says the LORD, thoughts of peace and not of evil, to give you a future and a hope." Jeremiah 29:11

Where Is the Good News?

By now I am sure you are asking - **"Where is this Good News you keep talking about?"** If our story stopped there, there would be no "Good News." Yet, in the midst of all that looked bleak and hopeless – God would make a way!

Here is the **"Good News."** God loved you and me so much that He made a way for us to escape death. However, for God to make a way for man, it would have to be in harmony with both His love and His justice. God is a loving God, but He is also a just God. He could not just wipe away man's sin. The penalty for man's sin had to be paid. The Bible reminds us again in Genesis 2:17 –

Good News!

> *"...in the day that you eat of it* (this fruit) *you shall surely die."*

Death was separation from God. It was not only a separation from the Garden of Eden, but it was also being eternally separated from God's presence. This was our plight - <u>unless something was changed</u>.

The penalty of death would have to be paid. Genesis 18:25 says,

> *"Far be it from You to do such a thing as this, to slay the righteous with the wicked, so that the righteous should be as the wicked; far be it from You!* ***Shall not the Judge of all the earth do right****?"*

Psalms 9:7-8 says,

> *"But the LORD shall endure forever; He has prepared His throne for judgment.*

Good News!

He shall judge the world in righteousness,
And He shall administer judgment for the peoples in uprightness."

God is a just God. He is a righteous God. The penalty of death had to be paid. Even though His love was extended to man, He could not wipe away the penalty of man's sin until that price was paid. Someone had to pay and overcome the penalty of sin. **Someone had to conquer death!**

Good News!

CHAPTER 9 REVIEW

ASK YOURSELF THESE QUESTIONS

1. What **kind of a plan** does God have for my life?
2. How does this plan show that **God loves me?**
3. Complete this statement – **"God's love demands** _____."
4. How is the way **God** deals with our sin **different** than the way **the world** deals with it?
5. What was **the penalty** that God was willing to pay in order that we might have a **future and a hope?**

Good News!

CHAPTER 10

"No one has power over the spirit to retain the spirit, And no one has power in the day of death. There is no release from that war, And wickedness will not deliver those who are given to it." Ecclesiastes 8:8

Who Can Conquer Death?

The million-dollar question is, **"Who can pay the penalty of sin and conquer death?"**

How many of you know anyone who will never die? When I ride my bike, I go by the Weatherford graveyard near downtown and see all the assorted marble tombstones. Every one of them represents a person who could not escape death (this is also true for the ones still alive who have purchased their grave-sites in anticipation of their death). I don't know anyone who will not face death. None of the great philosophers of this world have escaped death. None of the great religious leaders have escaped death. The grave of Confucius is still there, as is

Good News!

the grave of Buddha. People regularly visit these graves. They go on long journeys to see the grave of Mohammed.

But there is only one empty tomb - and that is the empty tomb of Jesus Christ!

So, to recap, man was totally incapable of paying the penalty of sin. Every man was conquered by death. Only God Himself could pay the penalty. Only He had the power to conquer death. **And God had a plan to do just that!**

Good News!

CHAPTER 10 REVIEW

ASK YOURSELF THESE QUESTIONS

1. Have you ever incurred a **debt you could not pay?**
2. When you could not pay your debt, **how did it make you feel?**
3. Has anyone ever offered to **pay off one of your debts?**
4. If you answered **Yes – how did this make you feel?**
5. What comes to your mind when you consider that **God Himself**, becoming a man in **Jesus Christ**, came to earth – **to pay off ALL of your debts (of sin)?**

Good News!

CHAPTER 11

"Let this mind be in you which was also in Christ Jesus, who, being in the form of God, did not consider it robbery to be equal with God, but made Himself of no reputation, taking the form of a bondservant, and coming in the likeness of men. And being found in appearance as a man, He humbled Himself and became obedient to the point of death, even the death of the cross." Philippians 2:5-8

A New Baby Is Born!

The only way God could pay our penalty and conquer death was if He became a man. So, as we continue our journey from Genesis to Revelation, the Good News continues. God decided to humble Himself and become a man. Jesus, the "Word of God," God Himself, became a man and entered the world as a perfect, sinless, baby boy. This is what we celebrate each Christmas. John 1:1 says,

> *"In the beginning was the Word, and the Word was with God, and **the Word was God**."*

Good News!

In Matthew 1:23 we read,

> *"BEHOLD, THE VIRGIN SHALL BE WITH CHILD, AND BEAR A SON, AND THEY SHALL CALL HIS NAME **IMMANUEL**," which is translated, **'God with us.'"***

John 1:14 goes on to say,

> *"And **the Word** (**was made flesh**) **became flesh** and dwelt among us, and we beheld His glory, the glory as of the only begotten of the Father, full of grace and truth."*

Jesus, God Himself, came and walked in our footsteps. He faced every temptation, difficulty, and experience of human suffering that is common to man. He did all of this as the perfect man, without failure, without sin. He did this so that He could pay our penalty and become the ransom for our sin. Finally, there was someone who could both understand our plight and free us from the power of sin and the sentence of death!

Good News!

Listen to Hebrews 4:15,

> *"For we do not have a High Priest who cannot sympathize with our weaknesses, but was in all points tempted like as we are, **yet without sin**."*

And Galatians 4:4-5,

> *"But when the fullness of the time had come, God sent forth His Son, born of a woman, born under the law, **to redeem** those who were under the law, that we might receive the adoption of sons."*

Matthew 20:28 goes on to say,

> *"...just as the Son of Man (Jesus) did not come to be served, but to serve, and to **give His life a ransom for many**."*

Good News!

CHAPTER 11 REVIEW

ASK YOURSELF THESE QUESTIONS

1. What did it **cost God** to enter this world as a human being?

2. Was Jesus merely a man, was He merely God, or **was He both God and man?**

3. Why did God have to **become a man** in order to pay the penalty for man's sin?

4. Did Jesus really **experience suffering and temptation** as a man?

5. What is the **main reason** Jesus came to earth? (Matthew 20:28)

Good News!

CHAPTER 12

"In Him we have redemption through His blood, the forgiveness of sins, according to the riches of His grace". Ephesians 1:7

We All Need A Blood Transfusion!

Have you seen the movie "The Passion of Jesus Christ?" Many have watched this movie, and in a profound and impacting way, they have learned about the death of Christ. They watched as Jesus shed His blood when he was mercilessly whipped and crucified. This is a very hard movie to watch. It is extremely intense, and many have criticized the Christian religion saying - "It's just a bloody religion." In fact, today some churches will not even sing songs that speak of the blood of Christ, like, *"There's Power in the Blood,"* *"There is a fountain that flows from Emanuel's veins,"* along with many others.

Many today ask, "What is the significance of the blood? Why did Jesus have to die? Why did He have to shed His blood for us?"

Good News!

Romans 5:9-11 says,

> *"Much more then, having now been **justified by His blood**, we shall be saved from wrath through Him. For if when we were enemies we were reconciled to God through the death of His Son, much more, having been reconciled, we shall be saved by His life. And not only that, but we also rejoice in God through our Lord Jesus Christ, through whom we have now received the reconciliation."*

Jesus came to **atone** for our sins. Atonement means that He came to secure for us a **formal pardon - not parole**. We are not on parole! As believers in Jesus Christ, we are not subject to parole officers. He came to give us a full and complete pardon. This means that He came to wipe away the complete record of our sin and shame. When we are pardoned through Jesus' death and resurrection,

Good News!

we receive forgiveness of sins, we are restored in fellowship with God, and all the guilt and its resulting punishment (death – eternal separation from God) is completely removed.

The price of atonement is blood.

We have seen from the Scriptures that the penalty of sin is death, complete separation from God, both physically and spiritually. Death is the opposite of life. The life of the flesh is in the blood. Therefore, the price of our atonement was a life for our death - the shedding of blood. Leviticus 17:11 says,

> "***For the life of the flesh is in the blood***, *and I have given it to you upon the altar to make atonement for your souls; for **it is the blood that makes atonement** for the soul.*"

This is true both spiritually and physically.

Good News!

In March of 2003, I underwent aortic heart valve replacement surgery. After the surgery, I was alive, the valve replacement was successful, but I was slipping away during my recovery because my blood count was rapidly dropping. The healthy blood cells were not being reproduced fast enough in my body. Everything else was correct, the artificial valve was sewn in carefully, and my heart was working properly. However, I was still drifting downward. I needed a blood transfusion!

Before I received this blood transfusion, I was unable to see clearly. My vision was blurry, and I was all alone. I can still remember it vividly. It was 10 o'clock at night when the nurse came in. She connected the bag of plasma (blood) to my IV, and I watched as the blood began traveling down the clear plastic tube toward my arm. Now, without any exaggeration – instantaneously, when that blood hit my body, it was as if all the lights had come on in the room. I could see! My blurry vision was completely gone! I had a new infusion of life!

Good News!

Such it is with the blood of Christ.

Good News!

CHAPTER 12 REVIEW

ASK YOURSELF THESE QUESTIONS

1. How do you feel when someone says – **"Christianity is a bloody religion!"**
2. What does the term **atonement** mean to you?
3. What is the **significance of the blood?**
4. Do I live my life **free from guilt and shame?**
5. Name **three things** that resulted from Jesus Christ's death on the cross.

Good News!

CHAPTER 13

"For such a High Priest was fitting for us, who is holy, harmless, undefiled, separate from sinners, and has become higher than the heavens; who does not need daily, as those high priests, to offer up sacrifices, first for His own sins and then for the people's, for this He did once for all when He offered up Himself." Hebrews 7:26-27

A Parking Meter...Or a Lifetime Pass?

God ordained blood (life) for the Atonement. In the Old Testament, animal sacrifices were given as a temporary means of atonement. It was like a parking meter. You had to keep feeding it or you would be in violation. The Old Testament sacrifices had to be repeated over and over again, as they looked toward a final payment that would be made in the future. Using the parking meter analogy, the final payment, instead of continually having to put coins in the meter, took place when the meter was removed, and we were given a lifetime pass!

Good News!

Jesus Christ, through His life and obedient death on the Cross, and through the shedding of **His innocent blood for our sins**, became the final sacrifice or payment for our atonement - **our formal pardon.** Hebrews 9:12 and 28 says,

> *"Not with the blood of goats and calves, **but by His own blood** He entered the Most Holy Place, once for all, having **obtained eternal redemption**…So Christ was offered once to bear the sins of many. To those who eagerly wait for Him He will appear a second time, apart from sin, for salvation."*

Jesus Christ has done it all! He has done it all! He paid the complete penalty for our sins through His shed blood. He has defeated sin! He defeated not only its penalty, but He defeated its power over our lives! Hallelujah! That's Good News! 1 Corinthians 15:3-5, 54-57 says,

Good News!

"For I delivered unto you first of all that which I also received, how that Christ died for our sins according to the Scriptures; And that he was buried, and that he rose again the third day according to the Scriptures: And that he was seen of Cephas, then of the twelve… So, when this corruptible shall have put on incorruption, and this mortal shall have put on immortality, then shall be brought to pass the saying that is written, 'Death is swallowed up in victory. O death, where is thy sting? O grave, where is thy victory?' The sting of death is sin; and the strength of sin is the law. **But thanks be to God, which gives us the victory through our Lord Jesus Christ**.*"*

Dear friend, that's **Good News!**

Good News!

That's **Great News!**

We can be restored to a loving relationship with God, and we can be freed from the penalty and power of sin and death through the blood of Jesus Christ, His atoning death for us.

But the question now is, **"How do we do it?"** How can we personally be saved from the power and penalty of sin and death?

Good News!

Good News!

CHAPTER 13 REVIEW

ASK YOURSELF THESE QUESTIONS

1. What **makes Jesus different** from the Priests in the Old Testament who offered daily sacrifices for sin?
2. **What was the sacrifice** that Jesus made?
3. Was Jesus' sacrifice enough to restore me to a **living relationship with God?**
4. Do I live my life like I am **fully pardoned** -*or* - **simply on parole?**
5. Do I really understand how to be saved from the **penalty and power of sin?**

Good News!

CHAPTER 14

"For He made Him who knew no sin to be sin for us, that we might become the righteousness of God in Him." II Corinthians 5:21

PAID IN FULL!

First, let me tell you what you cannot do. You cannot add anything to what Jesus Christ has done. Again, let me say it to you very plainly. **He has done it all!** It's a completed work, not a work in progress. When you try to add something (other than Jesus' death and resurrection) in order to obtain a right relationship with God, you're trying to do it through works. This is a losing proposition. You see, no matter how hard you try, no matter how good you are, you're never good enough to reach the level or standard of perfection that God requires. You are either perfect or you are not. God does not grade on a curve!

Good News!

There is only one person in life who lived to the standard of God's perfection. That person is Jesus Christ. You and I can't do it. **Jesus did it all!**

JESUS GAVE HIS LIFE! THE PENALTY FOR SIN IS –

PAID IN

FULL!

Good News!

CHAPTER 14 REVIEW

ASK YOURSELF THESE QUESTIONS

1. Is there **anything else** Jesus needs to do to save us from the penalty and power of sin?
2. What does **paid in full** mean to you?
3. Can I ever **be good enough** to have a relationship with God, and go to heaven, on my own efforts or merit?
4. Does God **grade on a curve?**
5. Who is the only person that **lived a perfect life?**

Good News!

CHAPTER 15

*"Jesus said to her, "I am the resurrection and the life. He who believes in Me, though he may die, he shall live. And whoever lives and believes in Me shall never die. **Do you believe this?**"* Jn. 11:25-26

How Can We Overcome Sin and Death?

As we have established, we cannot add anything to what Jesus has already done. Again – **He has done it all!** However, each one of us has to **personally respond** to what Jesus has done for us. There are only two responses that you and I can offer, and they are really simple. Let me give them to you.

The first thing we can do is **believe.**

John 3:16-17 says,

> *"For God so loved the world that He gave His only begotten Son **that whoever believes in Him** should not perish, but have everlasting life. For God did not send His*

Good News!

Son into the world to condemn the world, but that the world through Him might be saved."

The second thing we can do is **receive.**

John 1:12 says,

> "***But as many as received Him****, to them He gave the right* (power, ability) *to become children of God, to those who believe in His name."*

Good News!

CHAPTER 15 REVIEW

ASK YOURSELF THESE QUESTIONS

1. Is there anything we need to **add** to what Jesus has done through His death on the Cross?
2. Why did the Father send **Jesus into the world?**
3. What is the **first thing** we need to do in order to be saved from the power of sin and death?
4. What is the **second thing** we need to do in order to be saved from the power of sin and death?

Good News!

CHAPTER 16

"That (Jesus) was the true Light which gives light to every man coming into the world. He was in the world, and the world was made through Him, and the world did not know Him. He came to His own, and His own did not receive Him." John 1:9-11

Why Do So Many People Miss This Wonderful Free Gift?

Here is where it gets a bit blurry. This is really where people miss it. They do not understand...

What it means to <u>believe</u>.

How one responds in order to <u>receive</u>?

Today there is almost no context for a Biblical understanding of what it means to believe and receive. Many have heard people say, "Just <u>believe</u> in Jesus," or, "<u>Receive</u> Jesus into your heart." However, I have come to

Good News!

learn in my years as a pastor, most people do not really understand what these two things mean.

Believing and receiving is more than an intellectual acknowledgment of the facts. There are so many people today that believe in the general facts, but they still don't know Jesus. Did you know that the Bible tells us in James 2:19 that even the demons believe and shudder? And it goes without saying – there will not be any demons in Heaven! Surely everyone will agree that demons are not saved! So, believing and receiving is not simply an intellectual acknowledgment of the facts.

Believing and receiving is also more than simply saying, "I believe there is a God." Or, "I believe there was a man in history whose name was Jesus." Or, as many acknowledge, "I believe Jesus was a good teacher." This is not what the Bible is speaking of when it calls us to believe in Jesus and to receive Him as our Lord and Savior.

Good News!

<u>Believing</u> and <u>receiving</u> is when someone makes a total heart and life commitment to the Lordship of Jesus Christ. (Remember, Lordship means to rule.)

Let's take a journey back to the Garden of Eden. When Adam and Eve ate the fruit from the Tree of the Knowledge of Good and Evil, they were declaring, "I no longer choose to live under God's rule and authority. I'm going to do things my own way!"

When we come to Jesus Christ, we must be willing to put the forbidden fruit back on the tree.

We must be willing to turn from our sins and acknowledge our sinful nature. We must **<u>believe</u>** in and **<u>receive</u>** the Good News!

In other words, we must discover what it means to make a total life and heart commitment to Jesus Christ!

Good News!

CHAPTER 16 REVIEW

ASK YOURSELF THESE QUESTIONS

1. Were there people in **Jesus' day** who missed both who He was and why He came?

2. What are the **two reasons** people miss this free gift today?

3. Can a person accept the **basic facts** of the Good News regarding Jesus Christ and still fail to have a relationship with God?

4. What does it mean to you to **believe in Jesus Christ?**

5. What does it mean to you to **receive Jesus Christ?**

Good News!

CHAPTER 17

"Hypocrites! Well did Isaiah prophesy about you, saying: 'These people draw near to Me with their mouth, And honor Me with their lips, But their heart is far from Me. And in vain they worship Me, Teaching as doctrines the commandments of men.'" Matthew 15:7-9

Believing and Receiving is More Than Saying a Prayer!

You don't become a Christian simply because you say the "*sinner's prayer*"! You don't automatically have a relationship with God simply because you are born into a Christian family, or you believe in God, or you acknowledge that Jesus was a good teacher.

Each and every person must individually and personally invite Jesus Christ into his heart and life to be his Lord and Savior!

As you are hearing (reading) these words, **Jesus is knocking upon the door of your heart.** The Gospel of

Good News!

Peace, the **"Good News"** that began in the book of Genesis, now comes to its ultimate end with a **personal invitation** that is found in the last book of the Bible, the book of Revelation.

Revelation, chapter 3, verse 20 says,

> *"Behold, I stand at the door, and knock,* (the door of our hearts), ***If anyone hears My voice and opens the door****, I will come in to him, and dine with him, and he with Me."*

Please try and picture this in your heart and mind. There is a door upon your heart. This door only has one doorknob, and it is on the inside of your heart. Jesus is knocking on your door. Yet, Jesus will never break the door down. Why? Because Jesus will never violate your free will, the very gift that He gave you (and all mankind) in the Garden of Eden. There is no doorknob for Him to turn. There's only one doorknob, and your hand is on it!

Good News!

The only one who can invite Jesus into your life by opening the door of your heart - is you!

You are the only one who can turn that knob. Yet, you ask —

> **"How do I turn the knob?"**

> **"How do I open the door?"**

You do it through **three simple steps** that I am going to share with you right now in closing. These **three simple steps** are the keys to **<u>believing</u>** and **<u>receiving</u>**!

Good News!

CHAPTER 17 REVIEW

ASK YOURSELF THESE QUESTIONS

1. Is there more to becoming a Christian than simply **reciting a prayer?**
2. Can we say something **with our mouth** when we really don't believe it **in our heart?**
3. Do I sense that Jesus is **knocking on the door of my heart?**
4. Will Jesus simply come into my life, **or must He be invited?**
5. Am I ready to **turn the doorknob, to open the door of my heart?**

Good News!

CHAPTER 18

"Now I rejoice, not that you were made sorry, but that your sorrow led to repentance. For you were made sorry in a godly manner, that you might suffer loss from us in nothing. For godly sorrow produces repentance leading to salvation, not to be regretted; but the sorrow of the world produces death."   II Corinthians 7:9-10

The "Doorknob" is Repentance!

The *First Step* toward opening this door is to **Repent**. We must each personally repent of our sins.

What does it mean to repent? It's not simply saying, "Oh, God, I'm sorry." Most of the time, in all honesty, we are only sorry that we got caught, or we regret the consequences that have resulted from our sin. True repentance is when we are sincerely sorry that we have violated what God has told us. Repentance is acknowledging the fact that God alone is righteous, and that we are sinners in need of a Savior. This inward

Good News!

revelation brings us to the realization that - **We need God!** Now that is repentance!

Repentance is turning from our old way of life, acknowledging the fact that -

- **I cannot be my own boss.**
- **I cannot be the lord of my life anymore!**
- **My life is a mess!**
- **God, I need You! I need You in my life!**

When I was 17 years old, I moved out on my own into my first apartment in Fullerton, California. I thought I had it all together. I had a good job and a fast car. All of my life was before me. However, I was miserable and confused inside. I fought depression and wondered if life was even worth living. Miserable, defeated, and lonely, one night I knelt down on the floor in my apartment and cried - **"God, I need You!** If you don't come into my life right now, if you don't change me, I'm done with this life!"

Good News!

And there, humbly on my knees, something wonderful happened -

God came into my life in a powerful way!

Mark 1:14-15 says,

> *"Now after that John was put in prison, Jesus came to Galilee, preaching the gospel of the kingdom of God, and saying, The time is fulfilled, and the kingdom of God is at hand, **<u>Repent</u> and <u>believe</u> in the gospel.**"*

Good News!

CHAPTER 18 REVIEW

ASK YOURSELF THESE QUESTIONS

1. What does **godly sorrow** lead me to?
2. Is repentance more than merely **saying "I'm sorry?"**
3. What am I **doing** when I repent?
4. What am I **acknowledging** when I repent?
5. Am I ready to **repent and believe the Gospel?**

Good News!

CHAPTER 19

*"Now great multitudes went with Him. And He turned and said to them, "If anyone comes to Me and does not hate his father and mother, wife and children, brothers and sisters, **yes, and his own life also**, he cannot be My disciple. **And whoever does not bear his cross and come after Me cannot be My disciple.**" Luke 14:25-27*

Repentance Must Be Followed with Surrender!

The *Second Step* is to **Surrender**. We must be willing to surrender our will (our need to be "the boss") to the Lordship of Jesus Christ. This simply means that we must get out of the driver's seat and let Jesus take the wheel! We not only get out of the front seat and into the back seat – we also give Him the keys, the steering wheel, the registration, and our license!

We must surrender all!

Good News!

We are no longer going to drive solo. We are going to let Him drive. Everyone who has driven a car can relate to this. This is what it means to invite Jesus Christ to be the Lord of our lives. We allow Him to lead us, and His Word becomes our roadmap.

As I was on my knees crying, I said, "God, if You don't take control of my life right now, I'm going to do something really stupid. I'm going to ruin my life. **I need You to take control. Jesus take the wheel! I'm tired of driving.**"

2 Corinthians 5:14-15 says,

> *"For the love of Christ compels us; because we judge thus; that if One died for all, then all died; And **He died for all, that those who live should live no longer for themselves, but for Him** who died for them and rose again."*

Good News!

So, first I need to **repent**. I need to own up to my own sinful condition and my need for God.

Second, I need to **surrender**! I need to lay down my will and surrender to the Lordship (rule and direction) of Jesus Christ in my life.

Good News!

CHAPTER 19 REVIEW

ASK YOURSELF THESE QUESTIONS

1. What do you think of when you hear Jesus' call to **"…deny yourself, pick up your cross, and follow Him."?**
2. Jesus said we must be willing to count the costs of discipleship before following Him. **Am I willing?**
3. Who is sitting in the **driver's seat** of my life?
4. Can we simply surrender a **part of our lives** and still be a disciple of Jesus Christ?
5. Am I willing to let Jesus be the **Lord (ruler and king) of my life?**

Good News!

CHAPTER 20

"For with the heart one believes unto righteousness, and with the mouth confession is made unto salvation." Romans 10:10

Surrender is Lived Out Through Confession!

What is the *Third Step*? I need to make a **Confession!** I need to publicly confess Jesus Christ as my personal Savior and Lord, **verbally,** and through the **actions** of my life. And in this **third step,** we enter into the Biblical reality of **believing** and **receiving**!

This is not a call to put a Christian bumper sticker on my car or to simply say the "sinner's prayer" with someone. It is a call to **repent**, **surrender**, and **live my life daily as a follower of Jesus Christ!**

If Jesus Christ has really transformed my life, I need to let people know it. **I need to confess Jesus Christ as my Savior and Lord publicly through both word and deed!**

Good News!

And I need to remember that the way I live my life speaks louder than my words.

Romans 10:8-11 says, (my paraphrase),

> *"For what does it say, the word is near you. Right now the Word is right at the door of your heart. It's knocking, it's at the door of your mouth, upon the thresh-hold of your heart, that is what the Bible says.* ***It is the word of faith which we preach, that if you will confess with your mouth the Lord Jesus, and believe in your heart that God has raised Him from the dead, you will be saved****. For with the heart, man believes unto righteousness, and with the mouth confession is made unto salvation.* ***For the Scripture says whosoever shall call upon the name of the Lord shall be saved.****"*

Good News!

CHAPTER 20 REVIEW

ASK YOURSELF THESE QUESTIONS

1. **Complete this statement** – "I need to publicly confess Jesus Christ as my personal Savior and Lord, _____, and through the _____ of my life."

2. Is my life a **living confession (testimony)** of my faith in Jesus Christ?

3. To confess Jesus Christ is my Lord I need to live as a follower of Jesus Christ in both **word** and _____.

4. The Gospel message calls me to **repent, surrender all** to Jesus, and **live my** _____ as a **follower of Jesus Christ!**

Good News!

CHAPTER 21

"Behold, I stand at the door and knock. If anyone hears My voice and opens the door, I will come in to him and dine with him, and he with Me. To him who overcomes I will grant to sit with Me on My throne, as I also overcame and sat down with My Father on His throne. He who has an ear, let him hear what the Spirit says to the churches." Revelation 3:20-22

Jesus is Knocking!

Can You Hear It?

Please take a moment to reflect on the words that we have shared. Look back and reflect upon all that we've heard as we have explored the Gospel of Peace, the **"Good News"** from Genesis to Revelation.

I believe right now the Holy Spirit is speaking to many hearts to reaffirm a commitment which you have already made, as you embrace anew the importance of your

Good News!

commitment to Jesus Christ. Perhaps you've jumped out of the back seat and have climbed back into the front seat. **If that is so, simply repent and surrender to Jesus anew!**

Perhaps this is the <u>first time</u> you have really heard the Gospel of Peace, the "Good News."

You may have heard many of these words and terms before, but you never understood the complete Gospel message. **You realize that you have never seriously considered God's plan of salvation for your life!**

As we have explored the **"Good News"** together, it has felt like the words have been jumping off these pages and into your heart. For the first time in your life you are aware that someone is knocking at the door of your heart.

It is Jesus, and He is waiting for you to answer!

Good News!

You sense a strange tugging upon your heart. It is as if someone has taken a blindfold from your eyes. You sense a humbling recognition that you are a sinner and that you need a Savior. With a mixed sense of joy and humility, you understand why Jesus had to die. You understand why Jesus had to fulfill the righteous requirements of a just and holy God. And you now see that the blood Jesus shed was given to purchase your full pardon! **You stand amazed, realizing that Jesus has paid the full penalty for your sin!**

Now you know that His death and resurrection are not just a story that you once heard. This story, this **"Good News,"** has become a firm reality for your life! You know that Jesus alone can break the chains and the power of sin in your life. **You put your hand on the doorknob.**

You are ready to <u>open the door</u>!

You are ready to <u>believe</u> and <u>receive</u>!

Good News!

Just as I knelt on the floor of my apartment in Fullerton, California, right now, you can kneel wherever you are. With a **heart directed toward God**, in **sincere repentance**, and in **full surrender**, you can open the door as you proclaim,

"I need You, God!"

The doorknob turns when you recognize your need for Jesus!

To take this step of faith you do not need to pray a canned or lengthy prayer. All you really have to cry out is, **"LORD!"** It's as simple as that!

The Bible says — **"Whoever calls upon the name of the Lord will be saved."** And so, right now, just cry out,

"LORD JESUS, COME INTO MY LIFE!"

When we cry out to the Lord Jesus Christ and open the door of our heart through **humble repentance**, **personal surrender**, and **sincere commitment** when we Biblically

Good News!

<u>believe</u> and <u>receive</u>, Jesus Christ comes into our lives and we are forever changed! It is a change that brings true forgiveness, a full pardon, eternal and abundant life – for eternity!

Father, I pray for everyone right now who have called upon the name of the Lord Jesus Christ. I pray that You will come now and flood their hearts with the abundant reality of Your love. I pray that You will flood their hearts with Your presence. I pray that you will flood their hearts with the assurance of eternal life. I pray that through Your Holy Spirit they will know, that they know, that they know, **THAT THEY KNOW…**

They are now a child of God, through Jesus Christ their Lord!

What a *Great Day*! What a *Victorious Day*!

What *"Good News!"*

In Jesus' Name. Amen.

Good News!

Your Blessed Assurance of Salvation!

*"He who has the Son has life; he who does not have the Son of God does not have life. **These things I have written to you who believe in the name of the Son of God, that you may know that you have eternal life, and that you may continue to believe in the name of the Son of God.**"*
I John 5:12-13

Thank you for taking the time to read**,**

"Good News…
The Gospel of Jesus Christ"

If you have **believed** and **received** Jesus Christ as your personal Lord and Savior **for the very first time,** we want to encourage you to find a good **Church Home** that faithfully teaches the Word of God! Please visit with your local Pastor to discuss taking the next step of following Jesus Christ in **Water Baptism!**

God Bless You!
Pastor Kirk

Good News!

About the Author:

Kirk L. Zehnder is the founder of Resurrection Christian Outreach, and the former founding pastor of The Fellowship at Weatherford, a Foursquare Church in Weatherford, Texas. Pastor Kirk has been involved in both business and pastoral ministry for over 40 years. Kirk founded **Resurrection Christian Outreach** at the very beginning of his ministry to be a support ministry to help churches and individuals reach their full potential in Jesus Christ!

If you are interested in other resources from this ministry, or if you would like to secure a speaking engagement, please **email** us at: rcoutreach@aol.com

Or **write** to us at:
Resurrection Christian Outreach
2248 Addison Ave.
Clermont, FL 34711

Good News!

Acknowledgments

I wish to thank my **wife Karen** and **daughter Hannah** for always supporting and encouraging me in all that I do!

A special thanks to **Jackie Page**, who typed the very first transcript of this message.

To **Pat Watson**, Retired Educator, and anointed teacher. Thank you for doing the initial edit and critique of this book.

To my dear friend, **Pastor Steve Bontrager**, thank you for challenging me and helping me think through the final thoughts and construction of the closing chapters.

To **Dr. Sidney Westbrook**, thank you for being such an encouragement in my life and ministry. Your spiritual guidance and friendship mean so much!

To **Rick Wulfestieg**, former Director of the Children's Gospel Box Project for Foursquare Missions Press, thank you for your constant encouragement and mentorship.

To **Bob Hunt**, Director of Foursquare Missions Press, thank you for publishing our previous works - **"Jesus, Baptism, and Me," "Jesus, the Trinity and Me," and "Jesus, the Holy Spirit, and Me."**

Without all of you, this would not have been completed!

And most of all, thank you to my Lord and Savior **Jesus Christ** for Your life - which is the **"Good News!"**

Made in United States
Orlando, FL
28 August 2024